God's Adopted

Encouragement for Christians of all ages to grow-on...

By Victor Aramanda

Copyright © 4-17-2014 by Victor Aramanda

All rights reserved. No part of this publication may be reproduced, distributed, or transmitted in any form or by any means, including photocopying, recording, or other electronic or mechanical methods, without the prior written permission of the publisher, except in the case of brief quotations embodied in critical reviews and certain other noncommercial uses permitted by copyright law. For permission requests, send email to the publisher, addressed "Attention: Permissions Coordinator," at the email address below.

Please send requests or questions to info@godsadopted.com

Cover Design by Andy Taylor

First Edition

THE HOLY BIBLE, NEW INTERNATIONAL VERSION®, NIV®
Copyright © 1973, 1978, 1984, 2011 by Biblica, Inc.® Used by permission. All rights reserved worldwide.

These Scriptures are copyrighted by the Biblica, Inc.® and have been made available on the Internet for your personal use only. Any other use including, but not limited to, copying or reposting on the Internet is prohibited. These Scriptures may not be altered or modified in any form and must remain in their original context. These Scriptures may not be sold or otherwise offered for sale.

Scripture quotations marked (NLT) are taken from the Holy Bible, New Living Translation, copyright © 1996, 2004, 2007 by Tyndale House Foundation. Used by permission of Tyndale House Publishers, Inc., Carol Stream, Illinois 60188. All rights reserved.

Acknowledgements

Thanks: Thank You Father God, for adopting me and sending Jesus to save me. Thanks to my wife who has always supported my running after our amazing God and His ways even when people thought we must be crazy. Thank you to my friend and brother in the Lord, Richard Mull, who has always encouraged me to trust God, in this effort to write this book, or do anything that God makes clear as being part of His call on my life. Thanks to my chaplains in the 82nd Airborne Division for being God's key disciplers when I was first born again in Saudi Arabia during the first Gulf War, especially Bart Physioc and Bob Sinnet. Thanks to my family for always loving me no matter how crazy I seemed. Thanks to the following people who God chose to use to disciple me in His ways at various times in my life: Emory and Beverly Goodman, Joshua Goodman, James and Joy Hogg, Chaplain Bart Physioc, my friends and brothers at arms in the 82nd Airborne Division's All American Chorus, Richard and Dawn Mull, Len and Robin Harper, Peter and Fiona Horrobin, Andy and Cath Taylor, the leadership of Ellel Ministries and many others that I can't list due to lack of space....

About The Author

Victor Aramanda is the younger of identical twins. He was an air-force brat who grew up in the USA, Spain, Germany, Spain, and the USA in that order, was a parachute infantryman, was in full-time ministry for more than eight years, is a husband and father, taught many conferences, lead praise and worship, lived with his family in a missionary work in the UK and in the USA, has many skills and talents.

He received the spirit of adoption from God, was born-again, on September 16, 1990 during Desert Shield while he was an infantry paratrooper in the 82nd Airborne Division. Many things happened in his life during Desert Shield, Desert Storm as well as when he returned to the United States after the first Gulf War.

Table of Contents

Acknowledgements 3

About The Author 4

Table of Contents..5

Preface 8

Chapter One: A recent season in my own journey 10

   "I love you.", painful words?..10

   I never believed that God could help me like this... 13

   God wanted to give me a new meaning for "I love you." .15

Chapter Two: Get ready for this journey 18

   Prayer..18

   How to use this book 19

   The weigh-it, prove-it, and test-it factor............................20

Chapter Three: Beginning Steps 21

   The God that really cares for you, not a different one. 21

   Encouragement to enter into new levels of growth in intimacy and freedom..23

   Questions about God, as Abba as Father............................24

Head and heart assessment 25

Chapter Four: A Parable Based on Real Life 31

A dog named Spot 31

Before adoption 33

After being adopted 34

God adopted me 35

A lot like Spot 37

Chapter Five: What is your Christian age 40

What is your Christian age? 40

Problems I've seen 42

How do you grow 42

What's the big deal about age 46

Chapter Six: Preparation for Healing, or, stumbling block removal time 50

Stir up some thoughts 50

Confession, repentance 51

Exercise to help in preparing to learn more about forgiveness 52

Chapter Seven: A time to open a door for help and healing . 54

Forgiveness 54

What forgiveness does mean 58

What forgiveness does not mean 59

Unforgiveness 59

A time of prayer to actually apply and receive forgiveness 62

Chapter Eight: Growing-On..66

Help for individuals 66

A litmus test for all teaching and training before adding them as truths to live by 68

Chapter Nine: The most amazing person you can be 71

Be like Jesus, be who God made you to be.........................71

Conclusion...73

A closing prayer 78

Appendix..79

Speaking, Teaching, Training, and Questions 79

"Let's imagine", a resource for encouragement and self-belief-examination..80

Questions for more thought 81

Help for the church and its leaders.....................................82

Preface

So you have not received the spirit that makes you fearful slaves. Instead, you received God's Spirit when he adopted you as his own children. Now we call him, "Abba, Father." For his spirit joins with our spirit to affirm that we are God's children. (Romans 8:15-16 NLT)

Whoever does God's will is my brother and sister and mother. (Mark 3:35 NIV)

To the Jews who had believed him, Jesus said, "If you hold to my teaching, you are really my disciples. (John 8:31 NIV)

Now this is eternal life: that they know you, the only true God, and Jesus Christ, whom you have sent. (John 17:3 NIV)

This is a book written to encourage the children of God in growing especially if they have encountered growing pain along the way that stunted their growth in the Lord in the areas of being and experiencing what it is to have a living intimate relationship with their Abba Father.

This book is also written to help anyone who has been called to nurture, love and teach the children

God's Adopted
of God overcome some of the obstacles that may be hindering them from receiving the love and training which may have been being offered for years but not really being received.

Chapter One: A recent season in my own journey

"I love you.", was becoming more and more painful to say.

"I love you.", painful words?

Before getting into the teaching in this book I wanted to share a recent way that God, my Father in heaven, has brought some much needed healing into my heart. Ever since I began my relationship with God as my heavenly Father I have asked for help in understanding emotions. On this occasion He decided to help me with being able to say, "I love you." I was raised with several interesting rules about love and, "I love you." I was taught that I have to love my family, I didn't have to like them, or any decisions they make, or things they may have said, but, I must love them. Two appropriate times that it's right and good to say, "I love you.", are in parting and at the end of a phone conversation, because it may be the last opportunity you have to say those precious words. I began to try my best to apply what I believe were Jesus' teachings after I was born-again. I understood, "I love you.", meant that I was to love you with God's love and based on His definitions. Over time I also felt that part of loving meant to apply in my words and actions how I understood love to be. The most obvious explanation I can think of comes from the Bible. Love is patient and kind. Love is not jealous or boastful or proud or rude. It does not demand its own way. It is not irritable, and it keeps no record of being wronged. It does not rejoice about injustice but rejoices whenever the truth wins out. Love never gives up, never loses faith, is always hopeful, and endures through every circumstance. (1 Corinthians 13:4-7 NLT)

I never realized until recent years how my understanding of telling someone "I love you.", was becoming tainted. It had started to mean something to me that I didn't want it to mean. Instead of being a wonderful statement full of amazing meaning, deep within my heart it began to be painful. It began to mean that the hurt I perceived to come from a person I said it to, real or imagined, was automatically going to be forgiven with no consequence and perhaps little or no mention to recognize what had happened. So I would forgive, but then hold on to some resentment, not understanding that the resentment was growing and tearing me apart from the inside out. Over time

A recent season in my own journey

it started to be displayed in my lack of even using the phrase. I decided to stop saying, "I love you.", to several people. I had began feeling that whenever I said those special words that the recipients reacted as if I was saying something different, more like, "I want you to know you are forgiven if needed and now you can go ahead and cause me more pain. Also, I will just forgive you over and over again." It had taken on a meaning that was incorrect. I really like to be a man of my words and in time I started manifesting the messed up internalized meaning by my dwindling ability to even say the words to people who were close to me.

I went weeks with not saying "I love you.", to some of the closest people in my life including my wife. I could not say something I did not mean, (especially my internalized meaning). I stopped saying this phrase because it's meaning ultimately was that you were cleared from any wrong doing to me and now being given license to cause me pain again. The things that were causing me the most pain were not even being done intentionally, so these people who cared about me didn't even realize I was being hurt or offended. It just continued on and on. No wonder I had stopped saying the words, I was in self-preservation mode. I wanted to be able to say the

God's Adopted

words to my loved ones, but I could not agree with the meaning they had taken on. God's help came to me in an unexpected way through unexpected people.

I never believed that God could help me like this...

I never believed that God could help me using a twelve step program, much less that I could ever need one. The time finally came that I was ready to receive God's help on His terms instead of my own. Through books and conversations God made it clear that I was to go into a twelve step program for family members that had been affected by alcoholics. My first step father, who was very proud of being a drunk and an iron worker, had a greater impact on my life than I realized. A person who knows me asked, "How could your first step dad have had such a great impact on you since he was only your 'step dad' for three years?", as if to dismiss what God had made clear to me. I quickly repeated out loud as a response, this thought that had come to my mind, "A car accident can last only seconds and yet the trauma from those seconds can change a person's life forever." so that friend's comment was quieted. I had been in full time Christian ministry for over seven

A recent season in my own journey

years, had taught and helped many, many people in many different ways. So, here I was over forty years old needing help in an area none of my prior training had been able to fix. My pride was beginning to be revealed to me so that I could see it. Pride that I never realized the depth that I had, ouch! God used the twelve steps in many amazing ways.

God's instructions for me were clear, "Go through the twelve steps as I guide you. Trust in Me and that I am with you." I wasn't to leave my beliefs or stop trusting in Him, His words, or His ways. I was to allow my personal beliefs to be tested. Beliefs about myself, marriage and relationships. Beliefs about love, forgiveness, healthy boundaries, being controlling, and being judgmental. God used the program to give me an overhaul and some much needed healing.

I was taken out from all I understood so that He could teach me things He knew I needed to learn in a different way than what I had become accustomed to. I was not allowed to criticize or judge anyone else's beliefs, rather I was in need of help myself and this was His way of positioning me so that I could only receive instead of give. There are many things I could write about my experiences going through the the twelve steps and all the healing God brought to me through them, but the one I want to focus on here is about the words, "I love you."

God wanted to give me a new meaning for "I love you."

God wanted to give me a new meaning for "I love you." First He began to show me how His love for everyone is true and complete. He loves everyone with the same love He has for me, no more, no less. His love is so much that it's there when I do what is right according to Him or wrong. Whether I am good or bad. After a while I started to see how some people couldn't believe in God as I did and that God still loves them. They even could live in ways that I would feel are not pleasing to God and He still loves them. I am not speaking about salvation or adoption here, rather that the fact is Jesus died once for all. In the Bible we see, "But God demonstrates his own love for us in this: While we were still sinners, Christ died for us." (Romans 5:8 NIV) He cares and loves us all! We may not all chose His way or His provision for our lives or eternity, but He loves each of us completely. Even enough to allow us our free will to choose His way or our own. Back to the "I love you."

A new friend came to me one night and said, "I

A recent season in my own journey

Love you lots." He could see my lack of understanding and asked me if I had a problem with what he had said. I responded that in recent years I had not been saying that phrase very often at all. My friend then said that his meaning behind the words was sincere and simply meant that he cares about me, and hopes for only good to come to me and my life. When he shared his explanation with me I was impacted in a way I hadn't expected. Because of my friend's boldness and concern, my own painful meaning and understanding about the phrase was made clear for what it had become. It was distorted and wrong. God never taught that I could not feel, if anything the opposite. He never said that love demonstrated by forgiving meant I was to ignore pain and suffering, but that I was to learn to bring it all to Him. To learn healthy ways of dealing with the issues and pain with His help and by applying His teachings in my life. I was being given a chance to allow God to change my definition of what, "I love you.", meant to me deep on my insides. I could now choose to allow it to mean, "I care for you.", or as my friend shared with me, "I love you lots." This was an incredible change for me, I was able to begin saying, "I love you.", again without being afraid of putting myself intentionally in harms way by the words. (He also taught me healthy ways of dealing with the pain

God's Adopted
and frustrations, but those will have to wait for a different book.) God has a funny way of giving us opportunity to put His teachings into practice.

Shortly after being given a new definition for, "I love you.", I received a phone call from a cousin of mine who had never called me on the phone in forty years, she's like a great aunt to me. It was near Christmas time and my cousin said she'd called to ask me a few questions. "How are you and your wife doing?", "we are well", I shared. "When was the last time you told her, 'I love you.', or 'You are beautiful.'? You know that she needs to hear those things from time to time. When was the last time that you told your children that you love them?" She told me that I had been on her heart to call and that is why she'd called out of the blue with this encouragement. This would've been completely crazy if I never had known that God has a sense of humor and does these kinds of things some times. I was being challenged to begin saying, "I love you.", on a more regular basis to people I care about. Wow! My wrong belief was exposed and then changed by my willingness to allow it and my obedience to the process God had guided me to go through. He worked through people and His love through them. I am sharing this in hope that many people will want to get to know Him as their Father in heaven too.

Chapter Two: Get ready for this journey

Prayer

Heavenly Father I thank You and praise You for calling out to me through Your son Jesus, and I thank You and praise You for letting me hear You and helping me to hear from You even by Your Holy Spirit. Thank You for saving me, for making it possible for me to be born again, to be adopted by You as one of Your own. Thank You for passion and love and care for others, and for the desire to share Your truths and Your message from my heart that is being transformed by You. Thank You for continuing to heal me in every area of my life and that You are not done.

I pray for anyone who reads this, that You, Jesus, by Your Holy Spirit, will help them to receive anything and everything that they need to receive from You as a result of these words.

For you, the reader, I pray that Jesus would bless you and build you up and strengthen you and encourage you in many many ways. Also, I pray that He would confirm the work that He's doing in you along the way as you read. In Jesus's name I pray, amen.

How to use this book

Read, reread, and take notes, journal, write questions and thoughts and comments on the pages if you like. Ask God your questions out loud; tell Him your thoughts along the way. Ask Him to respond. Let this be a safe place and time to be real with yourself and with a loving and caring God, not any other. If you find yourself struggling to trust God in such a deep way then know this, "you are not alone.", "it can get better, give this process and its exercises a chance to be a part of the healing / growing journey for you and your life." My main reason for writing this book is to encourage and help others to give the God who is Love, the one who really does care about you, a chance, especially when something or someone, (even yourself), is trying to stop you. You are going to be O.K., please don't be afraid.

Get ready for this journey

The weigh-it, prove-it, and test-it factor

The things I share are from my heart and my beliefs, please test what I have to say. Keep what you like and leave the rest. I learned a long time ago that God is real and living, it is not my responsibility to prove that He exists to anyone, that is His responsibility. My responsibility is to share His truth in love and be the adopted child He's raising me to be, doing and saying what He leads me to along the way...His way.

Safety

Find a safe place and some safe time and read this book in safety. Give yourself permission to be honest with yourself no matter how strange it may seem. Do the exercises along the way if you want to, or however seems best for you at this time. I hope that this will be an encouraging and growing experience for you with the help of the best, greatest, most loving, most powerful, most amazing Father....God.

Chapter Three: Beginning Steps

The God that really cares for you, not a different one.

I've met a lot of people who are discouraged because they don't seem to be the good "children of God" they are being led to believe that they "should be".

A lot of these people are too hard on themselves and sometimes even the people they hope will be "lifting them up" seem to be "loading them down". (Often times unintentionally, well-meaning and in God's name). Many people have a terrifying image that comes to mind when hearing the word or name, "god" or "father". For them God is a very mean condemning, unforgiving, criticizing, un-trustable, going to-hurt you, doesn't really care about you, wants to keep you down, wants to scare you into obedience kind of god. No wonder they have a hard time calling on God for help. Please allow me to be

Beginning Steps

very clear, whenever I refer to God or heavenly Father in this book, I am speaking of the One who is actually: caring, loving, forgiving, wants to look out for you, is watching over you beyond what you can understand for good, is worthy of trust, made the only way in existence for you to come close to Him cause He knew you could never reach Him by your own power, better than the most loving human being ever....the true and only real God that I want to know more and more myself. In other words I only want to share about the good God.

I met a lot of people during the season of my life when I was in full-time Christian ministry which lasted several amazing years. Through those years I had the honor of being able to do, lead, and be a part of a lot of teaching, a lot of ministering, a lot of praying, and a lot of encouraging. I saw many people healed of emotional sorrows and brokenness, and even some people healed physically. It was most incredible to see many people grow spiritually. It was amazing and a blessing to be a part of how Jesus still trains up His disciples even in this day and age by His word and His power and His Spirit as well as His disciples loving one another as He loves them. It amazes and humbles me to see that He is able to use

God's Adopted us and our lives in every stage / state of growing as tools to help others, even as He continues His work in us.

I hope that this book can be used to strengthen and encourage you about the reality of what it is to grow as an adopted child of God.

I hope this can be a reminder for anyone who has made the choice to be adopted as one of His children to keep growing-on. Also, I hope this book can be an encouragement to the person who has been considering becoming born-again to go ahead and give this God a chance.

Encouragement to enter into new levels of growth in intimacy and freedom

Willing to be challenged?

I want to challenge you and I hope that you are willing. A lot of the answers and help this book is going to offer may be found in questions. Don't be surprised if you may actually hear more than one answer from your own mind and heart, or if you hear one answer in your mind that is different than the answer that you hear in your heart. Is it okay to hear a question and consider its answer inside and out? Is it

Beginning Steps

okay to be honest? Is it okay to not really know? Is it okay to be real? Do you want a real living God in your real living life to gain living hope and healing? I hope your answer is, "YES".

Questions about God, as Abba as Father

I encourage you to take some time and write your answers to each of these questions if you have the time.

Do you want a living relationship with the living God, really? Is your God more like your earthly father than you have realized? Could your beliefs limit how much you trust your God? Could your beliefs limit how intimate or emotional you can be with your God? Do you want more closeness with God? Does God look down on you when you have little faith? Does God hold it against you when you have doubt? Is it ok to admit that sometimes you have strong faith and sometimes you feel like you have weak faith? Do you feel like you know the, "correct", answers to most of the questions here but have a different answer as a faint whisper, or that you see your actions display which is different than your words in your mind? One of the toughest things I have seen people do is to put themselves in a place

God's Adopted

where they can be so honest that it's ok not to have to give the, "correct", answer if it's the honest answer in your heart. I have heard many times that the greatest distance ever traveled is that one between the head and heart. I hope to help that most worthy adventure with this book. Give yourself this opportunity. You are not alone in needing help and encouragement to continue growing.

Head and heart assessment

I wanted to include an assessment here for you to start this journey with a kind of land mark so that at the end you could see for yourself how you have been impacted. This isn't a test, there is no wrong answer or grade, it's simply meant to be a tool. I decided to do a portion here myself as an example. Please feel free to do one for yourself. You can write in the empty space in this book if you like or on a separate piece of paper.

Please join me in as I go through this process. Even if you don't actually write anything down, just take a little moment here and there along the way to pause and think.

Don't be afraid to be honest, actually please let me encourage you, "be honest!", (God already knows your answers in your heart and your mind and when they're different, He knew all of that about you even before this moment and He still loves you and still adopted you and still chose you and still wants to love you and still wants you to be able to grow on with Him.)

I will be considering what I think about my trust of God in several areas of my life and how I live-out my trust by giving a scale level of 1 to 10. I want to first note from my "head" a number representing how much I think and want to believe I can trust my God followed by a note of why. Next I will do the same thing based on how I feel in my innermost parts, my "heart", how much actually seem to trust God in that area whether big or small. My "head" represents my mind and intellect, what I think I should do, believe, and or think. My "heart" represents what I believe on the inside, what I seem to actually demonstrate or would demonstrate if I was not worried about what other people think or say, how I really feel and think no matter how right or wrong. The good, bad and ugly no matter how bad or ugly, ultimately just real and honest. Struggles in trusting God do not mean that I am evil or that I am ant-God or His ways, it means I still have growing to do. Because I consider myself a "child" of His, it's easier to accept that I don't have to know everything or do everything to perfection without ever making mistakes. Isn't it ok for a child to have to learn and grow?...Of course it should be understood and expected. Thank God!

Exercise:

List some areas I know that I struggle with trusting God, or areas I already recognize that I want to grow in trusting Him?

Finances, Relationship, Intimacy.

Scale of 1 – 10, 1 = little trust, 10 = great trust. 1 could mean I don't know or understand how to trust, or I don't want to trust or even I can't trust. Remember that this isn't about the "right answer", but about the "real" one inside. Now I will list the area, followed by my number representing the level of trust from my "head" followed by why and then the same thing from my "heart".

Finances:

Head(10), If He takes care of birds and bugs and provides their needs, how much more should it be true for me, a human being, the only thing in all creation created in His image, especially one of His children.

Heart(7), there are still times I don't know how I'm going to get free from some of the debts I have even though I have experienced a lot of His amazing provision through the years. There are still times I wish I could just win the lottery or something.

Intimacy:

Head(10), I know I should be able to share all my thoughts with God, just like I see demonstrated with King David in the Psalms in the Bible, he really shared what he really felt even when it sounded wrong and God still called him a man after His own heart. Amazing!

Heart(6) I resist exposing all of myself to Him out of fear of rejection. I know in my head that God knows everything already, but it's not the same as coming out with those things in conversation with Him. I look forward to being able to more and more.

Relationships:

Head(10) if I live in my relationships the way He says to then ultimately how the relationships go or don't, depends on Him and not me. If they depend on Him than the results will be the best and healthiest for me even when they may be painful at times.

Heart(5) I wish this number were higher, it has been in the recent past few years that God has shown me how I have been demonstrating a lack of trust of Him in my closest relationships. Instead of learning and trusting Him in being able to share what I really feel and think at times, or expressing my own anger in healthy ways when needed, I have been finding that I have been doing it my way...not His. I have been protecting myself by not sharing and speaking up in times when I think it could be uncomfortable. I have kept silent instead of trusting God to protect me especially when I needed to share something I thought or felt. There have been times I have kept silent instead being confrontational because I was afraid of how the other person may respond. Ultimately letting fear rule my relationships, instead of letting God rule and guard and protect my relationships. I can see now that I have taken the place of ruling. I have been acting like god instead of letting Him be God...and it shows.

It can be hard to be real sometimes, but there is hope! If I can expose and admit that I have these things, these struggles to myself then I can start asking for help. If I don't allow the truth inside to come out then help cannot reach it, not because it isn't being offered but because it's not being received. This can be hard. The next sections of this book will help in encouraging us to continue in the growing process. I say us because I am on this journey too. Before continuing, consider the following questions: What is God as you understand Him to be like? Is He approachable, why or why not? Is He distant, (for myself He was normally a great provider, but emotionally distant.)? Does He desire to spend time with you, why or why not?

Heavenly Father, I pray for Your help by Your Holy Spirit to give some special courage and strength to all who read this to be able to continue in this journey to grow closer to you. In Jesus' name I pray, amen.

Chapter Four: A Parable Based on Real Life

(This story is actually based on a rescue dog that my family adopted several years ago. The names have been changed, but this is a true story.)

A dog named Spot

One day there was a family that decided they really wanted a new dog, or rather an older dog that would be new to the family. They went looking and found a dog named Spot at a rescue shelter. Spot received a warm welcome to his new home and from his newfound family. Spot was well taken care of, he had food and water and treats and love and play and even a big yard. Spot lived in the house and was like a new member to the family. The father of the family found that there were certain things that must have been residual from Spots earlier life.

One day the father went out to get the mail and found a lot of the kind of junk mail that usually finds

A Parable Based on Real Life

its way into the garbage. Spot was playing in the front yard and when the father walked close-by Spot ran quickly away from the father and hid behind some bushes. The father had not done anything to hurt or scare Spot, but Spot sure acted as though he had. Remember, Spot was a rescue dog he had a history before this new family, a history that affected the way Spot thought and felt about life, about himself, about this new family, and about the world around him. Spot could not help but to live according to his own history and past, a past that affected his today. On a different occasion the father went out to call Spot to come into the house, there was a flag by the front door flying in the wind and when Spot came near to the front door the father noticed that Spot saw the flag flying and flapping in the wind and stopped in his tracks, turned, ran and then hid again. First the papers from the mailbox and now the flag flying in the wind, it was obvious that someone must have done something to Spot with loose stuff whether it was paper or material of some kind but the end result was Spot had definite fears of something bad happening whenever he experienced or saw things that reminded him of that past. It was going to take time as well as actual experience of safety and growing in trust for Spot to be able to fully enjoy being a part of a new family and a father that wasn't

God's Adopted

going to hurt him or miss treat him in anyway. The father had not done anything to deserve being treated the way that Spot was treating him. Spot was able to receive love and have fun in certain ways, but in other ways you could still see that Spot wasn't able to trust yet because of his existing inner scars, and fear that he learned in the past. It was going to take time, Spot didn't know this, but the father and Spot's new family thankfully did.

Before adoption

Before being adopted by this new family Spot learned a lot of things from the world that he grew up in. He learned that he couldn't always trust people, especially when they had things in their hand or if things were waving around in the air. As people we can look at Spot and his situation and understand clearly what was going on. We can easily say that it made sense that Spot acted and reacted the ways that he did because of his early mistreatments. His past taught him to take care of himself, to protect himself, to trust no one, especially people in authority.

A Parable Based on Real Life

After being adopted

After being rescued and then adopted some things changed for Spot but not others. Spot still needed to be taken care of, he still needed shelter and food and water. Initially when Spot was rescued he was taken out of harm's way, that is to say from continuing to be mistreated. That didn't mean that the effects of the mistreatment were taken away from Spot though. Spot had been rescued and removed from the place of mistreatment, but the effects of it were not so easily removed from Spot. Those effects would continue until Spots perspective on them, even individually for certain situations, changed. How many situations had there been? How much time would be needed for each situation to be healed? How could healing come? Who's responsibility was it to bring healing? Did Spot have a choice of how to respond to the many types of loving offers of help? Did he even have a choice whether or not to receive any healing?

We can see why the new family and the new father did not hold Spots reactions against him. They knew that it was going to take time for Spot to trust them in these areas that he was fearing them and his new life. They knew even at the time that they chose to adopt him that there were things that would take

God's Adopted
time. They knew that Spot had issues and they chose to adopt him anyway. They had chosen that they were going to care and love Spot because of whom and how they are, not because of whom Spot was before they knew him or how he was acting and reacting. From Spots point of view life was definitely better, but it didn't mean that everything absolutely had changed for him. Spot didn't know that he could trust these people completely. When he was fed he did not know if he was going to be fed again. Little by little, in time and with a step of trust here and one there and then again and again is how Spot would grow into this new life. Spot's ability to accept good things from his new family; things like healing, love, care, touch, concern, gentleness, patience and even kindness was going to take time. How long it was going to take depended greatly on Spot, and his choices whether or not to receive. The family already made the choice to adopt Spot, and to make time, and to give time, and to give love, and to give care, and commitment for Spot and to him.

God adopted me

It's amazing to me over the years how much I have noticed myself to be like Spot. There was a time in my life when I realized I needed help. I knew my

A Parable Based on Real Life

family and friends loved me and cared for me, but I also knew that they couldn't help me or that it was limited and partial help at best. I tried many different things to get help, but it seemed like depression and misery only grew inside and no help was ever coming. One amazing day as a parachute infantryman in the 82nd airborne division during the first Gulf War I became born again. One chaplain friend said it was as if I was just introduced to Jesus. I had followed a very simple prayer, something like, "Father God I believe that Jesus died for me to pay the price for my sins and I receive eternal life from You in Jesus's name and ask for your forgiveness of my sins, thank You for forgiving me. Please send Your Holy Spirit into my heart to guide me and lead me to follow after Jesus, in Jesus's name amen." It was very simple, and at the moment that I asked for forgiveness of my sins although it was not physical it felt like someone had lifted a heavy backpack off of my shoulders and in its place gave me peace inside my heart and mind for the first time. That was the moment that I became born-again, and was adopted into God's family. I now had my new Father in heaven. At that time, I asked Jesus to be Lord over everything in my life, absolutely everything. Looking back over the years I can now see that I was just a baby and as you grow and mature you find out that there are other things in your life that you didn't recognize when you were a baby, and couldn't because you were a baby, that need to be turned over to Him to take charge of and to be Lord over as you continue to grow and mature. Several years ago I was praying about how to teach people about some of these lessons and God showed me the story of Spot in a new way, as if I was Spot.

A lot like Spot

When God adopted me He knew I had plenty of issues. Issues from my past, and issues to come and issues to grow through in the future. He chose to adopt me even with all of these issues and He chose to love me and accept me completely as I was and in the state I was in at that moment. He knew that there would be times that I wouldn't trust Him, and couldn't from my perspective. He knew that it was going to take time for me to learn that I could trust Him, and for me to learn that He actually cares for me. He knew that sometimes I would do well in following Him. He knew there would be other times I would not do well in following. He knew that some situations I would never be able to trust Him in, at least not until years had passed by so that my experience could grow with Him. He knows that

A Parable Based on Real Life

there are still areas of my life that I have trouble trusting in Him today, and yet He loves me still! He knows that sometimes I run away from Him to receive comfort from my old ways of living, and that I try to protect myself by using my old ways of protecting myself or receiving protection and yet He loves me still! He knows that it takes time for a baby to grow and mature, even me, and yet He loves me still! He knows that there are other people in my life and around me that think I should grow faster and act better sooner and quicker, but I don't and yet He still loves me! I've learned and experienced over the years that I can trust Him for provision and taking care of me and my entire family! It has been easier for me to grow and learn that I can trust him for physical needs in my life; however, the emotional relationship has been taking a lot longer. He loves me still! He knows I don't understand love, and yet He loves me still! One of my many prayers is that He would teach me emotions from His point of view, that He would teach me how to love. Sometimes I do well in applying His teaching and others not so good, and yet He loves me still! It's as if He took me in as a baby and knew from the beginning that it would take time for me to grow, time for me to trust, time for me to learn, time for me to understand, yet He still loves me! Father God takes care of us much better than the

God's Adopted family in the story could take care of the adopted dog. If the adoptive family understood the time and effort it would take for Spot to recover, be healed, and receive their love, care, friendship, and kindness, how much more does our Father in heaven understand each of us! Is God okay with it taking time for me to grow? Am I willing to give myself permission to be a baby and to grow into maturity and for it to take time? How do we grow? It's like changing from an old way of being, acting and thinking to a new way.

A person who has been increasing and trusting God as their parent, is said to be growing "up". How can a person grow spiritually? Why does it matter if we consider ourselves grown, or at some level of growing? Could there be something significant about how we categorize people in our life as being a certain age? How does our perceived age of others and ourselves make a difference in our life? How about in our spiritual life?

Chapter Five: What is your Christian age

What is your Christian age?

What is your Christian age? What does this question even mean? The simplest answer might be thought of as the amount of time since you were born again, ultimately however, I'm speaking of the level of spiritual maturity that you are. Maturity isn't completely tied to a person's physical age. Have you ever been near an adult who is very immature? Maturity here is about a person's individual spiritual growth and how it affects all the areas of their life combined, body, soul, and spirit. A person who is said to be older spiritually could actually be younger physically than the people around them. A person's Christian age is mostly about that person's level of maturity and their growth in being an adopted child of God. One who acts like a child of God in the world that they live in, which includes a demonstration of transformation from the old way of life and living to the new. From living life as if they were God to living life allowing God to be their God. I know some people that could take some of the previous statements as being negative, condescending, or even belittling. Please don't! One of the reasons I'm asking so many questions is because I know that God is able to use them to stir up our thoughts, even deep beliefs that we may not even realize are there. It was only by allowing God to do this that certain areas of my own life are now being healed and made more mature, and restoration is taking place. I pray for all those things and more, for stumbling blocks to begin to be removed, for growth to begin progressing in areas that have been stunted, for freedom from having to be or act like someone God did not create you to be in the first place. Ultimately each person has to grow on an individual basis, being encouraged and nourished through that new relationship with God as having been adopted by a good heavenly father and also as they follow the Son being lead in the power and connection through the Holy Spirit. Also, it's important to have the fellowship of other believers. As simple as that may sound, many times I have spoken with people that are struggling against problems that they are not aware of. Is it possible to recognize that there must be a problem without being able to understand and identify what it is or all its

What is your Christian age

affects?

Problems I've seen

It isn't unusual to see spiritual maturity being treated like physical. Is it healthy to think that your spiritual age is directly tied to your physical age? Is it loving to hold a person to a higher level of responsibility and expectation then what would be considered age-appropriate? Is it possible that these kind of things are going on in the world that we live in? Is it possible that sometimes we ourselves are falling into these traps in how we deal with other people? Is it possible that sometimes we are placing these wrong expectations or judgments upon ourselves? How can you grow and become free unless you realize that these things are taking place in your life and around it?

How do you grow

Can you give yourself permission to be and act the age you are? Can you give other people the same permission? All of this requires some change in the way that you think, weigh, prove and test the things around you. You might find yourself having to turn away from people who are spiritually stunting your growth. I think it's important to mention here that most of the time when this is going on it's unintentional. I have heard and read teachings in the past that were well-meaning but not realistically helpful.

One example of how this happens is where a person is given a list of ways that they "have" to be without being given time to grow into "being" a person who could possibly be or act those ways. Does this sort of thing happen within spiritual relationships?

Several examples and scenarios to consider... A person joins a group, the group gives the person the list of 20 ways to be a good, or real Christian. Once the person is "taught" the list then they are expected to have learned it and held responsible to demonstrate it. Consider it this way, if we held a child of five years old to the responsibilities of a 30 year old it would be considered abuse or negligence or something wrong, as it should be!

How about this scenario, a person signs an agreement they are not really ready to agree to because they know they will be unwelcome otherwise, even though it's only implied and would

What is your Christian age

never be spoken as being the case.

    Another scenario: a person is born again. They are taught that they are a new creation and that the old has gone, the new has come and that they now have the mind of Christ. If this were said to a mature Christian who understands the fullness of the verses being referenced then that would be one thing, but it's being said to a baby who couldn't understand if they had to. Next they are brought into a situation where it's clear, but perhaps unspoken, that to be a part of the group that birthed them they must join. (Make a vow, sign a covenant, make commitments beyond what can be understood by a baby.). The baby then tries its best to act, and be the way they were told/taught that they must. As the baby fails at acting beyond their level of growth they find themselves in a dilemma. Fake it, or have to leave, but don't be honest to the fact that you are not able to live up to the expectations because there is no healthy acceptance or provision understood by the baby. The baby does not know that it will take time in various amounts for the various areas of need in its life to grow. Is it possible that those raising the babies don't understand these things are happening? They are part of what then results in the stunting of growth and development in

God's Adopted
some or all areas of many babies' lives. The babies then remain or leave not knowing any other course. Sometimes they put one area of life on hold from being developed while other areas still prosper. An example of this would be a person could be growing in the area of service while not feeling safe to expose an area of deep hurt, hidden sin, or pain that needs help.

What happens to the baby? They stay and do the best they can, they leave and find somewhere else to try to grow, or stop coming at all. They may fall away from any kind of fellowship in fear of experiencing more mis-treatment.

Do you think babies who experience failings of "doing" all the teachings, lists, and doctrines ever hold the failures against themselves in unhealthy ways, (things that were wrongly placed upon the shoulders of babies in the first place.)? Do you think the people that do these things to babies do them on purpose? Have you ever done or been a part of this unintentionally? Have you ever been around groups that did this in small or large ways? Has any of this sort of thing been done to you? Have you done any of this to yourself?

If a wound exists then it needs healing and help. I pray these things will be exposed so that healing can take place, not to re-live the past or pain, rather to allow the existing pain that began in the past to be uncovered. If a wound on my arm isn't exposed in a safe environment then it cannot be cleaned and taken care of in a good way to allow good healing to begin. I want healing for the babies in the church to begin as well as for anyone who helps in taking care of God's children to grow in this area if it's needed.

What's the big deal about age

I want to take some time now and focus on the perception of age and how it can unknowingly cause harm, or how it could really help us. We look around at people and automatically consider that person is old or young or older than someone else or older than us or younger than us and all of this has an effect on how each of us treats one another. It has a large effect on how each of us thinks about one another. It has a large effect on how each one of us judges or is critical of one another. It even has a large effect on how we judge and criticize ourselves. Physically speaking it's easy to understand how this can be very valuable and how our perception of someone's age can be a helpful thing. If I saw someone who obviously looked like a small child getting into a car and the car was running

God's Adopted
and they started to handle the controls, I might, rightly, try and take some action to stop a bad thing from happening. Many laws and consequences that we live by and obey are affected by our age. Some examples are the age that a person is legally able to purchase alcohol, or the age a person is legally able to marry, or legally able to make certain other binding agreements, and contracts. The idea of stereotypes and how we use them to live our lives isn't an altogether bad thing, but it's important to understand when they are used in a way that is harmful. I cannot ignore the truth and the value of understanding that a person who has lived longer than another person has had more opportunity and experience of life and therefore may have more understanding and even wisdom about life and living, or at least certainly they had more opportunity to acquire those things. Ultimately, I'm saying these things because I want to show how our whole understanding and perception about age and growth and growing in physical, emotional and intellectual terms is by default translated into how we think or understand about spiritual things. Not every part of a person matures at the same rate. The reason that our use of age in relating to others is overlooked is because we do it automatically. I'm not saying it's wrong, just that it needs to be taken off of auto-pilot so we can make

What is your Christian age

adjustments when necessary.

Your age and the age that you perceive someone else to be has a great impact on your life. Perhaps most upon how you treat others and what you expect of them. It may seem obvious, but that's exactly why it's often overlooked.

I believe that we are all composed of a body and soul and spirit. Also, that it's possible to have different levels of growth in each area. Is it possible that the different areas could have differing kinds of growth spurts each requiring different amounts of time to be completed? I view the "body" as being the physical, chemical part of a person, the "soul" as the mind, will and emotional part, and the "spirit" as the part of a person where we are alive or dead in actually having, experiencing, and being in a child/parent relationship with God. This is an adoption which ultimately depends on our choosing to enter into relationship with Him on His terms.

We have all been taught to have expectations based on a formula that is believed and acted upon, but rarely spoken about or challenged. The formula goes something like this: >Age = > maturity =

>reliability and trust. Think about it. If you see an older man or woman in church what kind of expectations do you have of them? Should they know the Bible? Can they be trusted with children? Are they going to be respectful? Are they more polite than younger parishioners, should they be? The problem isn't that we have or live by using stereotypes or taught expectations, but it if they go unchecked and we are never willing to test them then we become controlled by them instead of having them as helpful ways to quickly make assessments of people and life. Physical expectations do not always equate to spiritual, although there are certainly similarities we want to be careful not to become trapped unknowingly. To put it in simpler terms physical maturity does not guarantee a person's emotional or spiritual maturity.

All I'm saying is we need to give ourselves permission to test the different things that we think and believe and how it directly impacts how we deal with other people and how we allow them to deal with ourselves, perhaps most importantly how we deal with ourselves.

Chapter Six: Preparation for Healing, or, stumbling block removal time.

Stir up some thoughts

Here are some questions to stir up thoughts in preparation for the next section where we will focus on bringing the ways that many people are stunted in their spiritual growth into the light, or onto the table, so that freedom growth and healing can begin.

As I ask the questions, take a few moments just to think about your answers.

How old are you? When you read this question all by itself, what is it that you think of regarding your age? Is it mostly considering the physical? Let's try some more questions in a different way and with a little variety next.

The next questions are going to be regarding your body.

God's Adopted

How old are you? How long did it take for you to become the age that you are? How does your age affect how people treat you? How does your age affect what people expect of you? How does your age affect what you expect of yourself?

Now let's try the same thing but this time focusing on your soul, (mind, will and emotions).

Now let's try the same thing while focusing on your spirit, or spiritual life.

What are your thoughts when I ask you, "What is your Christian age?".

Confession, repentance

I learned a long time ago that to let God take over any area of my life often requires confession, repentance, and forgiveness. Confession is to acknowledge in the open how any ways or areas of past and present thinking, speaking, acting or believing are not in agreement with God and His way. Repentance is for the future and present, to turn away from the old way and turn/return to God's way. Forgiveness is the beginning so that release into God's love, care, freedom, rule and healing can start taking hold.

Preparation for Healing, or, stumbling block removal time.

One of the hardest things I have seen people from around the world struggle with is also one of the most important in growing as a child of God, forgiveness.

Exercise to help in preparing to learn more about forgiveness

On a piece of paper write a list of any person(s) or group(s) or institution(s) that you struggle with forgiving. Many people find that they need to be on the top of their own list, add yourself if you need to. I have found it helpful to stir up thoughts about forgiveness before trying to explain anything about what it is or is not.

Here is a simple exercise to help in beginning to identifying beliefs which make it a struggle to forgive. Lets keep it simple, just fill in the blanks, and create a new sentence with blanks, for each name you wrote on your list a moment ago.

I (circle one), [cannot / will not / am not able / don't know how] to forgive _____ for _____ because _____.

I know that sometimes I have to speak out or write out what I think to really recognize what I

God's Adopted
believe. Whatever is written on the blank line after "because" will be useful in identifying the belief about forgiving. Try and finish this exercise before continuing the reading.

Chapter Seven: A time to open a door for help and healing

Forgiveness

Most people I have ministered to over the years that have been struggling with forgiveness were stuck for the same reasons, ultimately reasons that proved they did not really understand forgiveness. There are many reasons I have heard as to why people don't want to forgive. Some people have wanted to punish themself or keep themself from receiving mercy or grace. I have heard people say that they don't deserve God's love, grace or forgiveness. Some other reasons I've been told are "I'm not worthy", or "people are still suffering as a consequence of my sin, how can I let myself have some relief?" There have also been people who punish themselves and resist God's forgiveness. Please answer this question if you struggle with being deserving or worthy of forgiveness. Can you name a

God's Adopted

time in your life that you deserved forgiveness? Think about that a moment..... It was a trick question, there is no such thing as deserving forgiveness, if there were it would be payment, not forgiveness. When a person says they will "forgive if..." or "forgive when...." They are not offering real forgiveness, they're making a deal of some kind. Forgiveness can never be earned or deserved. God gives forgiveness because of Who He is and out of His love for us, even when we don't understand. It's like He knows we don't understand and He loves us anyway. It's as if we're little children, but really, compared to God who is an adult? He loves us where we are at, thank God! Have you ever read "adults of God" in the Bible? No, of course not. At full age we are still children in position in His family, different ages from one another, but children to Him. Another major stumbling block that stops people from choosing to forgive is not understanding how consequences and forgiveness are separate issues. You can forgive, or be forgiven and still have a consequence remain even though you really forgave or were forgiven. Let me try to give some examples to help explain. If I lie to someone and they forgive me when I confess, is the trust still damaged as a consequence of what I had done? Yes. If the person who forgave me struggles with trusting me does that mean they did not really

A time to open a door for help and healing

forgive? No.

I have noticed that although a sin is forgiven the consequences that resulted from it are <u>sometimes</u> removed, sometimes they may linger, or sometimes they may never end while still in the life we live in this world. For example if trust being broken was a consequence it may take time for it to be restored, or it may never be restored. That is a consequence of the sin not the sin. The sin could have been forgiven and still have the consequence remain. I could have used an example of someone being forgiven of having sexual relations outside of marriage as a sin, but still had a consequence of a sexually transmitted disease which they carry the rest of their life. Yes, God forgave when they asked, and yes, the consequence remained. The consequence of sin does not prove anything about the forgiveness of the soul, rather it proves there was a cause, sin. Some consequences are worse than others just as the gravity, (how it can affect us and others), of some sins are worse than others. Any sin in my life creates separation from me and God in some way, and God will forgive any sin I confess and ask forgiveness for, however, the sin of lying could result in less trust while the sin of murder could result in the death penalty. Both are equally sin, yet two very different levels of consequence. We

God's Adopted
are misled if we think that there is no reason to consider what the gravity of a sin is when being tempted because we were taught all sin is just sin and can be forgiven without considering the sin with its consequences. I know in my own life it would have been better for me if I could have been careful to consider the consequences when I was being tempted to do things I knew in my heart were not right with God. My last example here will be from a testimony: On one occasion a person came to me wanting help with a situation of such high stress and anguish that it was tormenting them to the point of headaches and unrest. God made it clear that the root of their issue was unforgiveness. When I asked why they could not forgive and receive healing from God they told me that they knew that they could not forget what had happened. I restated what they were saying back to them like this, "so you are saying that if you could forget what had happened then you would be able to forgive?" they replied, "Yes, you have to 'forgive and forget', right?" I said, "No. you can forgive and still remember. The difference is that after you forgive you no longer are the judge of the people you forgave, God is. As judge you are trying to deem out and decide a verdict over their sin, only God can do that. You desire justice for the injustice and that is ok. You desire healing, if possible, of what is damaged and

A time to open a door for help and healing

relief of any pain and stress that is still present. Some things may be healed and some may not. You may even desire revenge, but God says vengeance is His. In order to forgive we must trust that God will handle everything about it including what may or may not happen to the other people."

The person thought about this, chose to forgive and then received healing from God. They now understood that forgiving is also a way God allows them to let Him be God over bad situations and things that happen in their life. They began to learn to deal with it His way instead of their way. By letting Him be God they could be a child who does as their Heavenly Father teaches along the way. So, forgiveness is not the same as trust or forgetting.

Let's look at forgiveness in another way.

What forgiveness does mean

Forgiveness means that you want to remove someone or group off of your list where you can be judge over them and put them onto God's, so He can be judge. Forgiveness means that you don't have to hold on to all the hurt and pain of what took place any longer so that you can expose, release and lift

God's Adopted
them to God and let Him begin His healing work.

What forgiveness does not mean

Forgiveness does not mean that you are ok or in agreement with something that was done or said. Forgiveness does not mean that you no longer desire justice in a situation. Forgiveness does not mean that you are giving license to more wrongs being done.

What forgiveness is not. Forgiveness is not equal to trust and forgiveness is not the same as forgetting. I can forgive and still remember. I can forgive and still be in a place that I do not trust.

Unforgiveness

I've heard unforgiveness described as, "giving yourself something that would hurt you while expecting the other person to feel the pain." Unforgiveness is like finding yourself locked in a prison cell filled with various levels of bitterness, resentment and pain because of what someone did or said to you. Being very angry with that person for keeping you locked in, while it turns out that you are the one holding the key that can open the door. One of the most difficult people to forgive can be

A time to open a door for help and healing

ourselves. Do you have any need to forgive yourself?

Forgiving yourself may need to be a part of your prayer. God can offer us forgiveness, but we don't have to receive it. Forgiving yourself is a way to allow yourself to be released from your own judgments of punishment. Have you been acting as your own Judge and god instead of allowing yourself to fall into the mercy and grace and love of the only true God? Whenever I try to be god over my own life it never goes very well. I admit that I'm not that smart. He's much more intelligent than I could ever dream of becoming...more than I believe any person can ever be. Is it any surprise that after having a more clear view of Him as a good God and Father, that I can now allow myself to receive love and mercy and grace from Him because I believe He thinks it is best for me, instead of me trying to take His place? As if I, as His baby or growing boy who has a limited view of life, could know better than Him, the good, all-wise, and most caring Father who really knows what is best. I want to encourage you to give Him a chance. I pray, Father, that You would confirm Your presence and goodness to the reader in some special way, in Jesus' name. Thank You, amen.

Jesus says that if we do not forgive others when they sin against us then our Father in heaven

God's Adopted won't forgive our sins. This can be really hard to believe when we are hurting, in pain, wanting justice and maybe even revenge. The truth is that God forgives us because of Who He is, not because we deserve it and then He calls us to forgive others as He forgave us. Our choice to forgive ultimately is a choice that is not dependent on the person we are forgiving or how we feel about the situation, rather based on God and His demonstration of His love toward us which is undeserved. We forgive now because we are His adopted ones allowing His love to be exercised through us as we obey Him with the help of His power working in and through us. Forgiving can be hard sometimes because it may seem that the person being forgiven will not have to receive any punishment or consequence for what they did that caused pain or injury, but really it is an exercise of trust. Can I trust that God will do what is best for me and the person I forgive, even though He may not let me know what He is going to do with the person after I release them to Him? Of course the answer is yes! God will always do what is best from His point of view, but from my <u>limited</u> point of view I may not know what that is or should be anyway. I once heard an old brother in the Lord say something that helps me trust God when I don't understand His ways or when I'm having a struggle trusting because I

A time to open a door for help and healing

don't think things are going to work out the way I want them to. "God's will for myself and my life is exactly what I would have it be if I knew everything about myself and my life that He knows." Think about that for a moment.

Next, I want to guide you in some prayer and pray for you in the next section. Please read it before actually praying out loud. If you agree with the prayer and are willing then please read it out loud with God's help.

A time of prayer to actually apply and receive forgiveness

[Prayer for yourself and life]

A Prayer to help growth, freedom and healing begin:

Heavenly Father, I pray in Jesus' name that You would guide me in my prayer so that Your healing and restoration can begin in the areas You are exposing by this teaching. Please bring to my memory anything I need to put into Your hands at this time.

[confession/repentance]

God's Adopted

I confess and acknowledge to You now any way I have taken part in mistreating your children, (take a moment and speak out any that He brings to mind.) I confess and acknowledge to You any way/s I have mistreated myself , (take a moment and speak out any that He brings to mind.) I now confess that there have been times that I wrongly _____, (others, myself...). (Take a moment and speak out anything that He brings to mind. Judged, condemned, criticized, wrongly accused, was unloving...) I confess that this was sin, I repent and pray for help in turning away from all the ways that are not Yours. Please help me to go Your way instead of any other.

[forgiveness, receive]

Heaven Father I now come to You needing to be forgiven of _____, (take a moment and speak out anything that He brings to mind...any sin, any way/s that you have been judging others or yourself). Thank You for forgiving me.

[forgiveness, give]

Heaven Father I now come to You needing to forgive _____ of _____, (take a moment and speak out forgiveness of any person/s and or institution/s that He brings to mind.).

[forgiveness, ourselves]

A time to open a door for help and healing

I now forgive myself of _____, (take a moment and speak out anything that He brings to mind.). Thank You for forgiving me. I now release myself and those I have forgiven into the freedom of Your forgiveness and pray for Your blessings upon them and myself, I also ask for Your healing, freedom and restoration to begin taking place, in Jesus' name, amen.

[My Prayer for you and your life]

Heavenly Father I come to You in Jesus' name and pray for Your blessings on my (brother or sister) and their life. In Jesus' name I take authority over anything that has been allowed to take hold or have effect upon my sibling's life and say that your right which came from unforgiveness is now gone because forgiveness has been given and received, so I command you in Jesus' name to release from my sibling and any area of their life you have been upon and go to wherever Jesus sends you right now. Jesus, I pray that You would come near now, even by Your Holy Spirit and begin to restore and bring healing in the areas that need it and fill any voids with Your Holy Spirit. Thank You Lord. Praise You Father God, in Jesus' name. Amen.

God's Adopted

[A Prayer to ask Jesus to come and rule over you and your life]

If God has shown you any ways that you have taken His place in your life then this prayer may be very helpful.

Jesus, I pray that You would be Lord over every area of my life, please send Your Holy Spirit to fill me and guide me in all Your ways. Thank You, Father, for adopting me and providing for me, in Jesus' name. Amen.

Chapter Eight: Growing-On

Help for individuals

Learn to weigh prove and test all things. Let God guide you by the Holy Spirit into all truth, whether you hear it or read it or however it comes. Run after the application of Jesus' teaching in your life. Is it possible that a well-meaning person can teach you something that you're not ready for? Of course! If it isn't time for you to apply that teaching then give yourself permission to fail or to say it needs to wait for a different time. Try not to condemn yourself or allow others to condemn you. Try not to take the place of the Lord, judge and God in your life, learn how to let Jesus be those things for you, not you yourself or even others.

I have asked many people this simple question. What has Jesus taught you? Have you ever heard that people have a "knower" and a "noggin"? One pastor I met used to say that you know when God has said something to you in your "knower" even though you may not understand it in your "noggin".

God's Adopted

I want to take a moment to talk about our "knower" versus our "noggin". Noggin is a word sometimes used to refer to the head, or brain or intellect. Saying you have a knower is another way of saying your innermost being, your heart and soul, the place where your deep rooted beliefs that you actually live your life by are located. You can know something in your head intellectually without believing it in your heart, the reverse is also true. You can also know something in your heart and head at the same time. It would be easier if we could simply replace all of the beliefs that we have deep down in our hearts with the truths that come from God. I think it becomes obvious when we look at our lives and how we act, respond, react and think that there are still other unhealthy beliefs down there. Beliefs that we need to give permission to God to show us, so that we can then choose His way or the old way that we're looking at, choose to exchange the healthy belief for our unhealthy belief. Transformation takes place more and more when we allow His ways, which are new to us, to replace our old ways.

I wonder how helpful it would be to consider making a list of what the Lord has taught you. Try and think of it this way, take whatever the Lord has taught you and live those teachings out in your life as best as you understand. Ask for His help and power in the areas you have trouble. In truth, we all need His help to follow His ways.

What about any other lists that are placed upon you? It is absolutely okay and encouraged to read or be taught ways to follow Jesus. Continue seeking to be his growing disciple and grow in your relationship as an adopted child of God. Just be careful, don't allow the teachings, or teachers to take God's place in your life. One old country song I heard long, long ago said something like, "the best sermon I ever heard was the one I saw." Jesus alone is your spiritual Judge, Lord and God! His rebuke and discipline come with love, mercy, and Grace. How can you tell if the teaching is from God?

A litmus test for all teaching and training before adding them as truths to live by

Common litmus paper is used to dip into water to check for acidity, it gives a clear result by changing color. Perhaps the answer to some simple questions I'll ask near the end of this story might be useful to you one day. I want to try to give an example of an time when I needed to decide whether or not a teaching and it's teacher were rooted in our heavenly Father.

God's Adopted

On one occasion I went to a big venue where many adopted children of God were being drawn to receive teaching along with signs and wonders. I was part of the leadership team of a ministry that people were calling and asking for direction of whether or not to go. I and two other pastors felt that we were to go as observers so that we could better pray how to respond to people looking to us for guidance. It was made very clear to us to observe and not participate. I felt several things as I watched and listened to what was happening: I felt at times that I was being wooed and tempted to be drawn in, that if I submitted to what the speakers were saying and doing that I would get what they had. I didn't see anything they had that I really wanted. I felt as if the Lord was telling me to look at all his sheep, how they had so much desire for greater things, but also how there was little discernment taking place. There were times that it seemed clear that the spirit ruling over the place was not loving towards the sheep of God at all, rather mocking and making fun of the sheep. The most obvious thing was actually that the love God has for His sheep, who He sent His Son to die for, was not present in the place. We left early, went and sat in the car in the parking lot and began weeping. We prayed for the people allowing this to happen and also for those leading and teaching as well. We prayed for the sheep, for our brothers and sisters and their leaders.

So, the test is simply "Is God in this? Is His love for His children being demonstrated? Are the people leading and guiding actually demonstrating the Lord's character and concern?" If I have a peace about any list or teaching then I can try and apply it in my life, otherwise I can put it down and trust God to remind me or give me the teaching again when it's time. The truth is that there are both good and bad teachers and teachings to be found. Two good ministries that do a lot of teaching that I experienced a lot of growth through in my own life are Operation Light Force and Ellel Ministries.

God used Operation Light Force in my life most powerfully to encourage me to trust Him and grow in faith. He used Ellel Ministries to give me a tremendous amount of long term training. At this time in the year 2014 I can say that both ministries have a lot of great training to offer. I recommend them to anyone who is looking for some solid teaching and training. Training and teaching that will help you in your growth in doing and teaching as Jesus did. Both of these ministries have a great deal of resources. Operation Light Force ,(www.operationlightforce.com); Ellel Ministries, (www.ellelministries.org)

Chapter Nine: The most amazing person you can be

The you God knows you to be now, the you He desires you to grow-on to become, and who you are on the journey between the two.

Be like Jesus, be who God made you to be

God in all His wisdom and knowledge determined one day to create you! Even more spectacular is this, He made you in His image. What does it mean to be made in His image though? People tell you that since you are a child of God that you should act like, and be like Jesus, but what does that even mean? I want to challenge you with some thoughts along these lines. God is bigger than I can imagine and His ways and thoughts are way beyond my reach. Please test what I am going to share.

I always thought when people shared with me that I was supposed to be like Jesus that it actually meant I had to stop existing and let Him take my place. As I continued to grow I found that God wanted me to allow Him to change me and my life to reflect the reality that I was now one of His children. In other words I was to allow His work to take place in His time and be His child as He intended me to be. To be "like Jesus" did not mean I needed to "be Jesus", rather, like Him.

Like a real child of almighty God, who acted like His Father exists and can be interacted with, spoken to, heard from, cared for by....like Jesus. Like a child of God who had been given gifts from heaven that impact His daily life, the way He interacts with people, the way He responds and prays and cares for others. Learning to be like Jesus in how He had an active relationship with His Father on a regular basis by speaking to Him through prayer. Learning to be like Jesus in how He knew the Word of God and understood it in a way to apply it's teaching in His everyday life as well as to help others. The way that he learned and grew in obedience and understanding and did as His Father made clear to Him. The way that He was filled and lead and comforted and counseled by the Holy Spirit. Does God intend for a person to be born-again so they stop existing or so that they can have eternal life? According to Jesus, eternal life is about knowing (relation-shipping) with God, (Father, Son, and Holy Spirit). Jesus says it this

God's Adopted way, "Now this is eternal life: that they know you, the only true God, and Jesus Christ, whom you have sent." (John 17:3 NLT)   As anyone follows Jesus and grows in their new position in life as an adopted child of the only true and living God it is bound to show in their life, and so is He.

Give yourself permission to become who God intended for you to be. His light through your life will impact your life and the things and people in your life more and more as you grow up in the Lord.

Conclusion

Give yourself permission, grace, mercy and love, to act your own age. Are you mature in the area of finance, then act like it, let it be demonstrated in your life. Do you have a hard time understanding and using emotions in your relationships, then let yourself have permission to grow and ask God to help you, and you will grow in His timing as He teaches you.

Give other people permission, grace, mercy and love, to act their age. Sometimes this means you have to let them act an age they don't even realize they are. Even harder, sometimes you may have to let them know they are not the age they are acting. This is done using the love, patients, and kindness you

The most amazing person you can be

would want someone to use upon you, if you were the one being confronted. Try to be forgiving of yourself and others who have been mistreating you. When you are given conviction and revelation that you have been mistreating others or yourself then remember confession, repentance and forgiveness. A good saying that I heard was "keep short accounts with God and man." Repent and stop. Praise God you can with His help! Continue in growing in your relationship with your Father in heaven. Keep asking for help in every area of your life. Pray, speak and talk to him out loud, no person has to hear you, but try it out loud. Even if it's a whisper it will be different than praying in your mind. If he is a living God then I want to encourage you to act like it's true, (I believe it is!). :-)

Read and study the Bible, find a translation you can understand. Who do you trust to ultimately give you understanding and guidance into God's truth's? Jesus, by His Holy Spirit. I have met several people who could not understand the translation of the Bible that they had and also felt wrong to try a different one because of teaching that they had received in the past. It's great that they were trying to follow instruction and help, but not so great that they could not understand anything they read. A person

God's Adopted
who cannot read Spanish may have difficulties if forced to only use the Spanish translation of the Bible. The point is, find a translation to read that you can understand and then test everything you read like everything else. If it helps, tell someone you trust who seems to be mature in the Lord to help you find a translation you can understand. If the only translation they offer is still not working then tell them. If they say you just don't have enough faith or something that makes no sense then find someone else to help you. There are things in scripture that will take time to understand, but if you cannot understand most of what you are reading, every-day kind of information, then there is a problem.

Have some regular Christian fellowship. Ask how God wants you to be a part of the body of Christ, the church. This does not mean a particular denomination. I have met people who I believe are Christians in many different denominations. Use the litmus test when trying to find a group to be a part of: Is God and His love for His people being demonstrated? Pray for God to help you to have people in your life who you can trust who also are on their own journey and growing in a relationship with God, one that began anew after they were born again. Ask them to share how they became an adopted child of God. Pray that you can have a safe person, or

The most amazing person you can be

persons in your life who you can share your journey with. Without having to be judged or condemned or criticized. Someone who can encourage you in the right direction and who you may even be a part of their encouragement.

Once a long time ago I thought that I was being unpleasing to God if I did not read the Bible every day. I had even heard teaching on several occasions that seemed to reinforce that belief. Even though I had read the Bible through and had years of study, there was a period of several weeks that I started to find myself reading only out of religious commitment. I would read and be disgruntled about it as if I was taking bad medicine or so that I could tell people that were "Bible reading police" in my life that I did my daily reading so they'd stay away from me with their judgments. I was reading for the wrong reasons. I was in a dilemma. I loved God and wanted to grow in understanding and knowing the Bible, but I did not want to read out of obligation alone. I wanted my reading to be an extension of my desire to spend time with God and sincerely wanting to to know Him and His thoughts and ways. Thankfully I had a friend who I respected, a pastor of a small church. I shared my dilemma with him and to my surprise and pleasant shock he did not condemn me or scold me. He actually shared something with me that I had never heard. He said that there were several men of God that he had great respect for who periodically would go through seasons of time of not having regular Bible reading. There have been plenty of times that I am grateful for men and women of God, fellow adopted children, who I could share my problems with in safety so I could receive love, kindness, and help. Safe people in my life who are on the same journey I'm on have definitely been a huge part of God's help for me to learn and keep growing to be who He is helping me to become.

Be who God is making you to be in his time. Give yourself and others permission to grow in the time they need. As you learn more then apply more. Live up to what you have already attained. If you haven't attained something then don't hold it against yourself, or be bothered if someone else tries to hold it against you. Forgive them, and or yourself and then keep growing on.

If you tried the assessment exercise near the beginning of the book then you may want to work through it again to see how God has begun to work in you already.

The most amazing person you can be

A closing prayer

I pray that God be close to you, that He make His face to shine upon you and that He bless you in every area of your life. In Jesus' name, amen.

Appendix

Speaking, Teaching, Training, and Questions

Victor Aramanda is an ordained minister with a BA in Communication and an MA in Clinical Christian Counseling. He has more than seven years experience in Christian teaching and ministry to both large and small groups of people as well as individuals. For information about speaking or teaching engagements or answers to any questions that you may have from having read "God's Adopted", please send your emails to, "info@godsadopted.com".

Appendix

"Let's imagine", a resource for encouragement and self-belief-examination

This is a section to use as a source for encouragement. Also it has helped me in a way to sometimes compare differences between my head verses heart beliefs. I've included it so that it may be of help to you.

Sometimes I like to consider the differences in my thoughts when I say "let's imagine" in front of phrases that I know in my head to be true, but need encouragement in my heart to be stirred up about what I believe as truth. When I read these statements I find that my head screams "I know this is true, it is not make believe, but real!", while sometimes in my heart I hear, "I want this to be true, Lord I believe, help my unbelief."

Let's imagine we have an enemy that we cannot see who's existence can be seen in the lives of people in this world and sometimes even our own.

Let's imagine that God is all-mighty! That there is none greater or bigger or better than my God!

Let's imagine that God can take care of us.

Let's imagine that God has a plan for us, a

God's Adopted future with peace, purpose and hope.

Questions for more thought

AW Tozer, "why does God ask any man a question?"

Is it ok to need help?

Is it ok for it to take some time to grow?

Is it ok for it to take less time to grow in some areas of trust and belief and more time in others?

Is it the adoptee's responsibility to "know" everything before having a chance to learn?

Should the adopted child be punished for what they have not been taught?

Should the new parent give their adopted child time to learn? Does the parent know that the time needed for each adopted child may be different?

Should the new parent give the adopted time to trust? Does the parent know that the time needed for each adopted child may be different?

Do you think the new parent knows that their adopted son or daughter can trust in one area while still not trusting in another? Do you think the parent holds that against the adopted?

Appendix

Did the parent know their adopted son or daughter had issues and problems that would take some time and experience to grow through before choosing their adopted child?

Is it possible for the adopted person to "feel" or "believe" something to be real or true in error? Should the new parent be expected to hold it against the child?

Help for the church and its leaders

If you lead or are a part of leadership in a place that provides teaching and support for God's children to grow and have found that there is room for change in this area of helping spiritually younger children of God grow then this section is for you. I certainly don't have all the answers, but I know that we pray more specifically for areas that are lacking if we are willing to let God show them to us. I believe that have a healthy fear of the Lord when it comes to teaching because He said that we as teachers would be judged more strictly, "Not many of you should become teachers, my fellow believers, because you know that we who teach will be judged more strictly. " (James 3:1, NIV). I write this book because He gives me peace to write what He has put on my heart and

God's Adopted conviction to trust Him with it and what He wants to do with it.

Allow God to guide you in making changes. Develop ways to allow people to grow and be encouraged to grow that are "spiritually" age appropriate. Let yes be yes and let no be no, be careful not to force people to make commitments that they know they can't keep or be judged for it when they later found out they couldn't. On more than one occasion I have seen and heard people being coerced into making unreal commitments by leaders who later judged them for failing. God holds the teachers to a higher level of responsibility. Learn to teach in ways that encourage and build up and strengthen instead of ways that force people to feel like they have to be who they are not. If we, teachers, are having difficulty loving and excepting God's adopted ones the way that he does then we need to give ourselves permission to admit it and ask God for His help. It can be very humbling. Find ways of turning the list of "how to be a Christian", and "how to really follow Jesus" into guides instead of laws. Become more like older brothers and sisters, elders, being willing to love and assist in Jesus' discipling of the younger instead of being judges and enforcers in the name of love without the presence of love. Learn to help the adopted of God, whom you are yourselves, to grow in

Appendix

the relationship and trust in their new adopted family. Especially how to grow closer and more intimate with Abba.

Learning and growing in the ability to treat people with understanding and expectations appropriate for their demonstrated ages may take effort and change. Treat a baby that makes messes with love and understanding and expectations you would have of a baby that is growing and makes messes. Learn and grow in being humble under-shepherds of Jesus, the One Good Shepherd.

If you need understanding or wisdom then seek and ask for it so that you can continue to grow into who God created you to be for His Beloved. As I am writing this book, I feel that there is a multitude of believers whose growth was stunted for one reason or another. It seems that a special season is coming where our love for one another, which comes from our Lord Jesus, will be used by our amazing Lord to begin bringing an unseen level of spiritual healing and maturing within the church, His body. A season for the world to know Jesus' disciples by their love for one another as not seen before. I do not have the full interpretation, just faith to write it down.

Father, I pray, in Jesus' name, for your healing and restoration to come to Your body so that Jesus'

God's Adopted name will be lifted high. I pray for the leaders and churches that desire to care for Your little ones to be blessed with strength and humility and love, that they would feel and know Your love for them and assurance of Your calling on their lives to be who You've made them to be for Your church. Father help them to be humble and repentant whenever needed and to receive Your forgiveness and blessings. In Jesus' name I pray, amen.

www.ingramcontent.com/pod-product-compliance
Lightning Source LLC
Chambersburg PA
CBHW071626040426
42452CB00009B/1512